ASK ISAAC ASIMOV

WHY ARE WHALES VANISHING?

BY ISAAC ASIMOV

HOUGHTON MIFFLIN

Boston • Atlanta • Dallas • Geneva, Illinois • Palo Alto • Princeton

2001 Impression

Houghton Mifflin Edition

Printed in China

ISBN: 0-395-78117-5

15 16 17-DBS-06 05

Contents

Words that appear in the glossary are printed in **boldface** type the first time they occur in the text.

Exploring Our Environment

Look around you. You see forests, fields, rivers, and oceans. You see plants, animals, trees, and birds. All of these things make up our **environment**. We share the environment with all other living things. But sometimes we cause problems for the creatures with which we share the environment. For example, because of our actions, many different kinds of whales are dying out. Why is this happening? Let's find out.

Amazing Creatures of the Depths

Whales are among the world's most amazing animals. The largest whale, the blue whale, is bigger than the biggest dinosaur. Its heart is the size of a car. Its tail is at least as wide as a person is tall.

Although whales live in water, they are not fish. They are **mammals**, like you and me. Whales give birth to live young and care for one another when they are sick or in danger.

6

Whales with Teeth and Whales Without

There are two main types of whales: those with teeth and those without teeth. Toothed whales are closely related to **dolphins** and **porpoises**. Toothed whales eat mainly fish.

Whales that don't have teeth have **baleen**. Baleen is a bony material that forms thin

8

plates which hang from the whale's mouth. With baleen, a whale can strain shrimp and other tiny animals from the water. It opens its mouth and takes a huge gulp of water. When it closes its mouth, it pushes the water out through the baleen. The animals the whale eats get caught on the baleen's jagged edges.

Why People Have Hunted Whales

Since prehistoric times, people have hunted whales. They ate whale meat, melted down whale fat for fuel, made baleen into fishing rods, and carved whale teeth into buttons. As shown here, some people who live in arctic regions still hunt whales to feed their families. They kill very few whales.

But most modern **whalers** kill whales to sell them. Whale oil is used in soap, candles, and machine oil. Whale meat is used for pet food. These things can be made from other materials. But people still keep killing whales. Methods of hunting whales have changed so much that many types of whales are **endangered**. These whales may die out.

Whaling, the Old-fashioned Way

Whaling used to be a very risky business. Whalers went out in small boats that a whale could easily flick over with its tail.

Whalers used to hunt whales with hand-held
harpoons. Each harpoon was attached to the
boat by a rope. If the whalers hit a whale,
the whale would dive, dragging the whalers
on a rough and dangerous ride. Hours later,
the whale floated to the surface, exhausted.

Whaling, the Modern Way

Whaling the old-fashioned way was so difficult that many whales escaped the hunters. Until modern times, whales thrived in the world's oceans.

People hunting whales today have a much easier time catching them. They chase whales with motorboats. They shoot them with harpoons that explode inside the whales. The dead animals are towed to factory ships, where the meat and oil are removed. With these modern methods, people have killed one-fifth of all the whales.

15

Oceans of Problems

The use of modern whaling methods is only one reason why whales are dying out. **Pollution** is slowly poisoning some whales. Fishing nets trap other whales or prevent them from reaching their feeding grounds.

Low **populations** also cause problems for some types of whales. Only 3,600 right whales still swim the seas. These whales may have a hard time finding each other in the vast oceans. That means the whales cannot **breed** easily. This lowers the right whale population even more.

Saving the Whales

People have recognized that whales have been in trouble for many years. Since 1946, many nations have agreed to limit the numbers of whales they kill. Killing whales that are endangered, including the right whale and the blue whale, is not allowed at all.

Many countries have banned all products that contain whale meat, whale oil, whale teeth, or other whale parts. But not all countries follow these practices. Thousands of whales are still killed every year.

How Can You Help?

Many different groups are working to help whales survive. Some groups try to get governments to ban whaling. Other groups try to protect the whales directly. For example, members of the organization Greenpeace follow whaling ships as they stalk whales. If a whaler aims at a whale, Greenpeace members go out in a small raft and float between the whalers and the whale. You can help whales survive by joining any of the groups that work to protect whales.

STOP

GREENPEACE

Making the World Safe for Whales

Even if people stop hunting whales, these creatures still may not survive. Whales need clean, safe places to live and raise their young. Unless we stop polluting the oceans and blocking them with fishing nets, the whales may die out. The whales will probably survive only if we start taking better care of the world we share with them.

22

More Books to Read

Whale Magic for Kids by Tom Wolpert (Gareth Stevens)
Whales and Dolphins by Francene Sabin (Troll)
Whalewatch! by June Behrens (Childrens Press)

Places to Write

Here are some places you can write to for more information about whales and what you can do to help them. When you write, be sure to ask specific questions and include your full name and address so they can write back to you.

Greenpeace Foundation
185 Spadina Avenue, 6th Floor
Toronto, Ontario M5T 2C6

Greenpeace USA
1436 U Street NW
Washington, D.C. 20009

Center for Marine Conservation
1725 DeSales Street, Suite 500
Washington, D.C. 20036

World Wildlife Fund
1250 24th Street NW
Washington, D.C. 20037

Glossary

baleen (buh-LEEN): bony material that forms plates in a whale's mouth; used for catching small, floating animals for food.

breed: to mate and give birth to offspring, or young.

dolphin (DOLL-fin): a mammal related to the whales that is smaller than a whale. Most dolphins have beaklike snouts.

endangered (en-DANE-jurd): at risk of dying out completely.

environment (en-VIE-run-ment): the natural and artificial things that make up the Earth. The oceans are part of the environment.

23

harpoon (hahr-POON): a long spear used in hunting.

mammal (MAM-uhl): a type of animal that has hair and feeds milk from mammary glands to its young; most mammals are born alive rather than from eggs. Both whales and humans are mammals.

pollution (puh-LOO-shun): the addition of harmful dust, liquids, or gases to the environment.

population (pahp-yoo-LAY-shun): the number of animals or plants in a group. The population of whales has greatly declined in the twentieth century.

porpoise (PORE-puss): a mammal related to the whales that is smaller than a whale. Most porpoises have blunt snouts and triangular fins.

whaler (WHAY-lur): a person who hunts whales; anyone who kills whales for money.

Index